Contents

Introduction

Part I: The Celts

Introduction

Said the druid, "The child that shall be brought forth tomorrow at sunrise...shall surpass every child in Ireland." -The Book of Lismore

Brigid was born at sunrise on the first day of February. Her mother gave birth in the doorway of their home, "neither within the house nor without."[1]

The story of Brigid's birth is filled with symbolism. She is born as the day breaks and as the night comes to an end. And this isn't just any day. It's February first, the pagan festival of *Imbolc* which celebrates the end of winter and the beginning of spring. She is born upon the threshold of her home. Her mother has one foot inside the house and the other outside. The story suggests that Saint Brigid was born at a time of change and in the midst of two different worlds.

This event occurred sometime in the middle of the fifth century AD when Ireland itself was experiencing great change and was, like Brigid, on the threshold of two worlds. On one side was the old world of Celtic paganism with its Druids, warriors, and tribal chieftains. On the other side was the rapidly growing world of Roman Catholicism led by a charismatic bishop now known as Saint Patrick. It is a fascinating time in Irish history and no one personifies this period better than Brigid.

This book is both a history of Ireland during Brigid's lifetime (from the mid fifth century to the early sixth century AD) as well as a biography of the saint herself. It begins by examining the Celtic people, their way of life and their pagan beliefs. This includes a detailed look at the Celts' religious leaders, the Druids. We'll then deal with the conversion of Ireland to Christianity and the unique nature of the early Irish Church.

The remainder of the book will be an in depth examination of Saint Brigid's life, the founding of her monastery at Kildare, and the lasting impact she has had on Catholicism both in Ireland and throughout the world.

Part I: The Celts

Who were the Celts? I defy anybody to say. – G.K. Chesterton, Heretics

"Nowadays, we are, in the interests of History, recording facts with such conscientious passion that we are making the writing of history impossible."[2]

This quote is taken from Professor H. D. F. Kitto's excellent book *The Greeks* published in 1951.   Since then the "conscientious passion" for recording facts has done more than simply make history writing difficult.   It has, in many ways, sucked the life out of history.

Nowhere is this more apparent than with the history of the Celts. Consider the following quotes from some of the subject's most prominent authors:

- *"To believe that we can penetrate the Celtic mind, and share the Celts' psychological condition and feelings, is a pure waste of time." – Stuart Piggot* [3]

- *"The whole use of the terms Celt and Celtic is something which should be avoided as it distorts our understanding of the archaeological record." – John Collis* [4]

- *"The Ancient Celts of Britain and Ireland are an essentially bogus and recent invention." – Simon James* [5]

So, according to these scholars, we shouldn't attempt to understand the Celts at an emotional or human level. That would be "a pure waste of time." Nor should we refer to them by the name Celts...because that might confuse things. In fact, maybe we're foolish for even believing the Celts existed at all in Britain or Ireland.

Nothing about these quotes (including their authors' condescending tone) encourages us to keep reading. It's a shame because the Celts did indeed exist and they were some of the most interesting people in Western History.

Chapter 1:
Celtic History

The Celts originated in central Europe in present-day Austria and Switzerland. The earliest evidence of their culture was found in Hallstatt, near Salzburg, where archeologists unearthed a Celtic cemetery dated to around 700 BC. The cemetery was comprised of over a thousand graves containing artifacts from all aspects of early Celtic life: weapons, pottery, jewelry, etc.

These early Celts had a well-developed material culture. They had grown wealthy by mining iron and salt and trading these items for wine and other commodities throughout the Mediterranean.

Around 650 BC the Celts began to spread rapidly across Europe, becoming well known to the Greeks and Romans. Ancient Greek writers referred to them as *Keltoi* while the Romans knew them as either the *Celtae* or *Galli*. They crossed to the British Isles sometime after 600 BC where they were, according to historian John Davis, "powerful and confident enough to be culturally dominant."[6]

By 387 BC the Celts waged war against the Romans and burned their city down. In 279 BC they ransacked the sacred Greek temple at Delphi. The Greek writer Strabo tells us that "the whole race...is war-mad and both high-spirited and quick for battle."[7]

Things started to change for the Celts in the late third century BC as Rome began building its Empire. First, the Celts of northern Italy and parts of Spain were conquered. Then Rome invaded and subdued southern France. By the late 50's BC, troops lead by Julius Caesar had defeated the united Celtic tribes of Gaul and claimed the entire province for Rome.

In 43 AD, Emperor Claudius ordered the Roman army to invade Britain and colonize the island. This was easily done in the southern territories. But Celtic warriors in the Highlands of Scotland were able beat back the Romans and halt their expansion in the early 80's AD.

By 120 AD the Emperor Hadrian stopped Rome's expansion into the north of Britain and built a massive, seventy-mile-long wall near the current border of England and Scotland. Hadrian's Wall became a boundary line between the Roman Empire and the Celtic world for nearly 300 years.

The largest tribe in Britain during Rome's invasion was the Brigantes. The tribe took its name from the Celtic goddess Brigantia, *Brig* meaning "High One". A similarly named goddess, Brighid, was revered in Ireland. As Rome established itself in Britain many Brigantians fled to Ireland. These immigrants quickly assimilated with the Irish Celts and their two deities—Brigantia and Brighid—were merged into a single goddess named Brigid. This goddess was the namesake of Saint Brigid and many of the stories connected with the goddess would later be attributed to our Saint.

Rome never invaded Ireland but at least one Roman general contemplated the idea. The general's name was Agricola. He commanded Rome's legions in Britain from about 77 to 84 AD and his son-in-law was the famous historian Tacitus.

Tacitus wrote a biography of Agricola's service in Britain. In it he recounts,

I have often heard Agricola say that Ireland could be reduced and held by a single legion with a fair-sized force of auxiliaries; and that it would be easier to hold Britain if it were completely surrounded by Roman armies, so that liberty was banished from its sight.[8]

Agricola even had an Irish prince in his retinue to assist with such a task. Nevertheless, neither Agricola nor any other Roman official followed through on an invasion plan and Ireland remained the only part of the Celtic world to entirely escape colonization.

The Roman Empire began to decline in the late second century. According to one of its writers, Cassius Dio, "our history now descends from a kingdom of gold to one of iron and rust."[9] By 407 AD the Western Emperor, Constantine III, withdrew troops from Britain in order to help defend Rome from barbarian attacks. Just three years later, in 410 AD, his successor, Honorius, sent letters to Britain's major cities informing them that Rome was no longer able to defend the island and that its inhabitants must fend for themselves.

After Rome withdrew from Britain many aspects of Roman culture were preserved by the Catholic Church. Catholicism officially reached Ireland and its Celtic people in 431 AD when Pope Celestine sent a bishop named Palladius to the island. Although this first attempt of Christianization was unsuccessful later missionaries, especially Saint Patrick, had great success in converting the Irish.

As Ireland embraced Christianity it began to experience a cultural awakening. With astonishing speed the island was transformed from a land of savage, pagan Celts to "the Isle of Saints and Scholars." It was during the early stages of this transformation that Brigid was born.

Chapter 2: Celtic Character

Although the early Celts were spread throughout continental Europe and the British Isles, they shared a number of characteristics that made them distinct. They had a common language and material culture. They had a unique physical appearance and temperament that ancient writers found remarkable. The Celts also held religious beliefs that their contemporaries often considered strange and terrifying. To fully understand the Celtic people—the people Saint Brigid lived among and ministered to—each of these characteristics should be discussed in some detail.

Celtic Language

Many modern writers believe that the most satisfactory way to classify the Celts is through their language. As author Norman Davies puts it, "The story of the Celts is rooted in language. For the Celts were, and still are, a conglomeration of peoples speaking a series of related languages. They are a linguistic group, not a national, ethnic, or racial one."[10] This view was shared by ancient Greek and Roman writers who had no problem generalizing the Celts based solely on their language.

The Celtic language emerged sometime around 1000 BC throughout the British Isles, the Gaulish coastline, and parts of central Europe. Its emergence and prevalence were due to commerce within these regions. The Celts acted as middlemen between Mediterranean merchants and the peoples of the north and west. They facilitated the movement of wine, salt, jewelry, weapons and most other commodities sold throughout Europe. Thus the Celtic language became an early *lingua franca* for traders across the continent.

But the language did more than facilitate trade. It helped strengthen and unify the Celtic peoples' social values, political beliefs, and religious practices.

Over time many of these Celtic-speaking regions were conquered by the Roman Empire. The Celtic nobility and the upper classes within Celtic society sought to win favor and status with Rome.

To do this they adopted Roman customs and began replacing their Celtic language with Latin.

The Roman historian Tacitus describes how the Celts of Britain embraced the language and habits of their new rulers:

Instead of loathing the Latin language they became eager to speak it effectively. In the same way, our national dress came into favor and the toga was everywhere to be seen. And so the population was gradually led into the demoralizing temptations of arcades, baths, and sumptuous banquets. The unsuspecting Britons spoke of such novelties as 'civilization', when in fact they were only a feature of their enslavement.[11]

This "Romanization" of the Celtic people was far more thorough and lasting on the continent than it was in Britain where Roman rule did not establish itself until 43 AD. In the few Celtic areas that managed to avoid Roman conquest, the Celtic tongue survived. These areas include modern-day Wales, northern Scotland, and all of Ireland.

Although Ireland was never subjugated by Rome, its people still heard the Latin language spoken by merchants from the Empire who made frequent visits to the island. Such interaction would have happened long before Ireland's exposure to Christianity.

Brigid, who was born in the middle of the fifth century AD, would have lived in an increasingly bilingual world. She would have used Latin when practicing and administering the Catholic faith. But Celtic was most likely her native tongue and she would have used the language colloquially when interacting with her family and her community.

Material Culture

The Celts were excellent metalworkers who decorated their weapons, jewelry, and luxury items with distinctive images and geometric patterns.

Some of the earliest and finest examples of their metalwork were discovered in Switzerland in the 1850s. The items discovered had been produced by Celtic people around 450 BC. These Celts and the remarkable items they created are referred to as the *La Tène* culture.

In his book *Who Were the Celts?*, author Kevin Duffy gives an eloquent assessment of the *La Tène* culture and the Celts' artwork throughout their history:

It was a highly original, abstract form that was not an accident in just one locality. The numerous surviving examples of this new style appear on weapons, body ornaments, horse harnesses, chariot equipment, and drinking vessels that have been excavated from sites across the entire width of Europe. Dazzling in the complexity of its design, it has been compared to modern abstract art, yet it is uniquely different, developing in a style unlike that of any other contemporary culture.[12]

The Celts retained this style of artwork for almost 1,500 years. It was certainly familiar to Irish churches and monasteries in Brigid's time and it was used by them to embellish their buildings and to illuminate their Bibles and other manuscripts. Probably the most famous example of such work is the *Book of Kells* produced by Celtic monks sometime around 800 AD.

A similar manuscript known as the *Book of Kildare* was produced at Brigid's monastery. The twelfth century writer Gerald of Wales saw this book on his visit to Ireland and gives us the following description:

Among all the miracles of Kildare nothing seems to me more miraculous than that wonderful book which they say was written at the dictation of an angel during the lifetime of the virgin. This book contains the concordance of the four gospels according to Saint Jerome, with almost as many drawings as pages, and all of them in marvelous colors. Here you can look upon the face of the divine majesty drawn in a miraculous way; here too upon the mystical representations of the Evangelists, now having six, now four, and now two, wings. Here you will see the eagle; there the calf. Here the face of a man; there that of a lion. And there are almost innumerable other drawings. If you look at them carelessly and casually and not too closely, you may judge them to be mere daubs rather than careful compositions. You will see nothing subtle where everything is subtle. But if you take the trouble to look very closely, and penetrate with your eyes to the secrets of the artistry, you will notice such intricacies, so delicate and subtle, so close together and well-knitted, so involved and bound together, and so fresh still in their colorings that you will not hesitate to declare that all these things must have been the result of the work, not of men, but of angels.[13]

Sadly, the *Book of Kildare* was lost or destroyed sometime after Gerald's visit.

Physical Appearance

The Celts were incredibly vain and obsessed with their physical appearance. By all accounts both Celtic men and women were tall, well-built and muscular. They had long red or blonde hair, blue eyes, and fair skin which the Greeks praised as being "milk-white". According to the Roman historian Ammianus Marcellinus, writing in the fourth century AD, "all of them with equal care keep clean and neat and...no man or woman can be seen...in soiled or ragged clothing."

Obesity was punished in Celtic society. Strabo tells us that the Celts "endeavor not to grow fat or pot-bellied, and any young man who exceeds the standard measure of the girdle is punished."[14]

Celtic men whitened and spiked their hair using a chalky substance called lime-water. They shaved their body hair and, at least in Britain, tattooed themselves with blue ink made from woad.

Noble men grew long mustaches that often covered their mouths. "Consequently," says Diodorus, "when they are eating, their moustaches become entangled in the food, and when they are drinking, the beverage passes, as it were, through a kind of strainer."[15]

The Celts wore bright, colorful cloaks that they embellished with tartan patterns. These cloaks were often fastened with an iron or bronze brooch at the shoulder.

Unlike the toga-wearing Greeks and Romans, Celtic men favored pants known as *bracae* ("breeches") which covered their legs entirely.

Women wore long skirts which wrapped around their waists and extended down to their calves. The skirts were made of tweed woven with bold check patterns. Such garments have been found by archeologists in Denmark and Austria.

Celtic women loved jewelry. They wore enameled bronze bracelets and anklets as well as torcs around their necks. Some wore necklaces made from glass beads or coral.

They grew their hair long, wore braids and used pins to hold together elaborate hairstyles. Make up was also common among Celtic women. This included nail polish, blush and eye-shadow. Apparently Celtic fashion trends spread to the ladies in Rome. In 20 BC a Roman poet named Propertius criticized his mistress and other Roman women who used cosmetics as "aping the painted Briton."

It's uncertain how Saint Brigid dressed. It's possible that she wore the simple garments of a nun. However, some writers suggest that Brigid dressed in the same robes worn by women of the druidic order. In some cases this would be a solid white or black robe. But there are instanes of more colorful and elaborate druidic vestments. In the *Cattle Raid of Cooley*, for instance, the Irish druidess Fidelma is described as follows:

> *She wore a speckled cloak fastened around her with a gold pin, a red embroidered hooded tunic and sandals with gold clasp. She had hair in three tresses; two wound upwards on her head and the third hanging down her back, brushing her calves. She had a light gold weaving rod in her hand, with gold inlay.*

Temperament

Ancient writers describe the Celts as being fond of alcohol and violence. In war it was customary for individual Celts to step forward before battle and challenge the bravest man in the opposing army to single combat. The challenge was usually made along with insults and derisive gestures toward the enemy lines.

Celtic warriors decapitated their victims and kept their severed heads for display. According to Diodorus:

When their enemies fall they cut off their heads and fasten them about the necks of their horses...they carry them off as booty, singing a song of thanksgiving over them. These first-fruits of battle they fasten by nails in their houses, just as men do in certain kinds of hunting with the heads of wild beasts they have killed. The heads of their most distinguished enemies they embalm in cedar oil and carefully preserve in a chest, and these they exhibit to strangers.[16]

If the Celts were not fighting foreigners they fought amongst themselves—even at their own feasts. During their public dinners the bravest warrior in the tribe was permitted to take the best piece of meat. Disputes often arose over this privilege and men fought to the death to establish their primacy.

Much of this fighting was fueled by alcohol which the Celts relished. Some in the wealthy classes drank wine imported from Italy or Marseilles. But most Celts drank beer made from wheat and occasionally flavored with honey. The beer would be poured into a common cup and passed around a group of Celts as they sat upon the ground or rested on cushions made of wolf skin. The merriment would continue until the Celts "filled the whole region with their wild singing and horrible and diverse yelling."[17]

Many considered the Irish to be the most savage and gluttonous of all the Celtic people. In fact, the first-century geographer Strabo even accused them of incest and cannibalism. Although he admits that he had "no trustworthy witnesses" for these claims

Chapter 3: Celtic Gods and Religion

Despite their wild behavior the Celts were deeply religious. Julius Caesar described them as excessively devout. They saw a spiritual side to nearly every aspect of life. Every stream, mountain, well and grove had its own spirit.

Initially these spirits did not have a human form. The Celtic leader Brennus visited Delphi in the late fourth century BC. When he saw the Greek gods carved out of stone he laughed and mocked the Greeks for believing that the gods resembled men.   This changed by the time Caesar invaded Gaul in the first century BC.   He frequently observed wooden statues among the Celts. These statues represented their gods and goddesses having both human and animal forms.

According to Caesar, "the god they worship most of all is Mercury and his statues are numerous...After him come Apollo, Mars, Jupiter, and Minerva. These they regard pretty much the same as do other nations."[18]

It was common for the Romans to equate foreign gods with their own. This was done for two reasons. First, the Romans considered their gods to be supreme beings who ruled universally. They refused to believe that Roman gods shared their attributes with foreign deities. For instance, the Roman god Jupiter controlled lightening and was often represented grasping a thunderbolt. The Celts also had a god of thunder named Taranis. The average Roman would reject the idea that lightning and thunder were commanded by one god in Italy and another in Gaul. Thus the two gods must be one and the same.

The second reason Romans merged foreign gods with their own was to encourage assimilation. After conquering a foreign land the Romans could either suppress the native religion or permit it to exist alongside Roman beliefs. Whenever possible the Romans favored allowing conquered people to keep their religious practices. This approach helped maintain peace within the Empire and often resulted in the Romans mingling their religious rites and beliefs with those of conquered nations.

A similar approach was used in Saint Brigid's time. As the Catholic Church spread throughout Europe, it frequently showed great tolerance for pagan religious customs and even incorporated many of them into Catholicism.

The gods of the Celts may have shared many attributes with Roman deities. But they were certainly not the same. The Celts had over 300 gods and goddesses. The most popular deities were members of the Celtic pantheon known as the *Tuatha Dé* ("tribe of the gods"). Below is a summary of the most prominent members of this pantheon.

Dagda

The "father of the gods" was Dagda, a powerful but kind deity who was associated with magic, wisdom, fertility and banquets. He is often depicted as a large, jovial man with a full beard and a short tunic that doesn't completely cover his back side. There is a comedic aspect to this god that some believe was added by later Christian scribes.

Dagda had a number of magical possessions. He carried with him an enormous club which could kill several men with a single blow. The handle of the club, however, could restore life to the dead. He also owned a golden harp that flew to him whenever he called it. When Dagda played the harp the seasons would change. Finally, as the god of banquets,

Dagda carried a magic cauldron which never ran out of food.

He was married to the battle goddess Morrigan and together they produced the goddess Brigid. According to myth, Dagda first saw Morrigan as she was bathing in the River Unshin in County Sligo. Morrigan was nude and her long, red hair was braided into nine tresses. Dagda immediately wooed the goddess and shortly thereafter Brigid was born. The place where this meeting supposedly occurred is known as the "Bed of the Couple."

Morrigan

She was the goddess of war. Her name meant "Great Queen" and the Irish believed that she intervened in battles to protect and aid those she favored. She appeared to warriors before or during combat in the shape of a raven. Those who saw the bird knew that death was imminent but they did not know who would die.

Like many Celtic deities, Morrigan was often represented as three goddesses in one. Her daughter Brigid was also depicted as a single entity comprised of three separate goddesses. The number three was sacred to the Celts. And the ancient Irish would have readily accepted the idea that three supernatural beings could make up a single god or goddess. This belief would later aid Saint Brigid and other Catholic missionaries as they taught the doctrine of the Holy Trinity.

In addition to her role in war, the stories of Morrigan frequently contain elements of fertility and sexuality. The most famous of these stories is told in the *Cattle Raid of Cooley* when Morrigan appeared before the great warrior Cuchulain as "a young woman with a dress of every color about her and her appearance was most surpassing." Morrigan spoke to the hero saying "I have loved thee for the high tales they tell of thee." But Cuchulain was focused on war and he rejected her advances saying "Not good is the time thou has come."[19] After this rebuff, Morrigan promised vengeance on Cuchulain. He later dies in battle and Morrigan again appears before him. This time she lands upon his corps in the form of a raven.

Brigid

The Celts believed that three sisters, all named Brigid, forged together to create this goddess. This could explain why Brigid has so many attributes. She is the goddess of learning, healing, and poetry. These traits made her highly regarded by the Druids. The Celts relied on Brigid to guard their sacred wells and ritual fires. She also protected livestock, crops, newborn babies and their mothers.

According to author Brian Wright in his book *Brigid: Goddess, Druidess and Saint*, Brigid was "a purely Irish goddess"[20] conceived by Druids in Ireland between 71 and 74 AD.

Just prior to her conception, the Romans invaded and conquered most of Britain. The largest tribe in Britain at that time was the Brigantians. This tribe took its name from its patron goddess Brigantia. Many Brigantians and their druid priests fled Britain after the Roman invasion. They sought refuge in Ireland where they began to assimilate with the Irish Celts. Part of this assimilation involved merging the Brigantian deities with those of the Irish. The Irish had at least one goddess (Brighid) with a name similar to Brigantia's. The two deities also shared common characteristics such an association with sacred wells and a connection with farming and livestock. Thus these goddesses were merged together by the Druids in an effort to unite the Irish Celts with the immigrating Brigantians. The result of this merger was the goddess Brigid.

The Celts identified Brigid with their festival of Imbolc. This festival was held on the first day of February and it marked the beginning of spring. Imbolc was seen as a time of cleansing and renewal. Many Irish brought their livestock indoors with them throughout the winter. During Imbolc these animals were moved back outdoors and home windows and doors were opened to air out the dwellings. Women would stand in the open doorways of their homes and pray for Brigid's blessing for spring.

One Imbolc tradition involved using wheat or reeds to make a doll of the goddess Brigid. The doll, known as a "biddy", would be placed on a bed of ashes in the home's hearth along with a symbol of male fertility such as a stick or a wand. The objects were left there over night. If the ashes were disturbed the following morning, it was a sign that the coming spring would be fruitful and prosperous.

Like many pagan festivals, Imbolc would be adopted by the Catholic Church and celebrated as the Feast of Saint Brigid (February 1) and Candlemas (February 2).

Belenus

Belenus was the god of agriculture. He also embodied the sun and its restorative powers. Images of Belenus have been found throughout the Celtic world. He often appears with a female consort who is thought to be Belisama whose name means "the Brightest One."

The great festival of Belenus was called Beltane. It was celebrated on May 1 and marked the beginning of summer when cattle were driven out to pasture.

The festival involved bonfires that the Celtic people and their cattle walked around in order to protect them from disease and misfortune. All fires within a community would be extinguished and relit using the Beltane bonfire. During this festival the Celts also decorated themselves, their homes, and their livestock with yellow flowers which represented the summer sun. Food and drink were part of the celebrations and libations were poured out to the fairies and spirits that the Celts believed were present at the festival.

Belenus was even popular among the Romans who equated him with the Greek god Apollo. Emperors Diocletian and Maximian each had Belenus's name inscribed on monuments in Italy during the late third century.

Lugh

The god Lugh was praised by the Celts as a warrior, a poet, and a craftsman. His name (pronounced *loo*) means "the shining one" and his status throughout the Celtic world is shown by the number of cities and counties that bear some variation of his name. These include Lyon in France, Louth County in Ireland, and Leiden in Holland. London is a Latinized version of the original name Lugdunum which meant Fortress of Lugh.

He fought with weapons that were both indestructible and unstoppable—a sword named *Fragarach* ("the answer") and a spear called *Areadbhair* ("the slaughterer").

He was accompanied by his ferocious hound, *Failinis*. The dog is described in the *Book of Lismore* as "That hound of mightiest deeds, Which was irresistible in hardness of combat."[21] We're also told that the dog's fur had the power to turn water into beer or wine.

On August 1 the Celts celebrated *Lughnasadh* or "Lugh's Assembly." The festival marked the beginning of the harvest season and it was celebrated on top of hills and mountains. Many Celtic tribes declared a day of truce for the event and competed with each other in sports and games. They performed a dance depicting Lugh's battles with rival gods in which he won the harvest for mankind and vanquished famine from the Earth. As Christianity spread throughout Ireland many of the activities enjoyed during *Lughnasadh* became Catholic traditions and some of Lugh's achievements were later attributed to Saint Patrick.

The Festival of Samhain

No discussion of Celtic religion is complete without mentioning Samhain— the fire festival marking the end of summer and the beginning of winter.

Samhain took place from October 31 to November 1. During the celebrations it was believed that the doors to the "Other World" were opened and the dead roamed among the living throughout the night. As part of the festivities, the Celts wore animal masks and went about their villages reciting verses in exchange for food or other treats.

The Romans incorporated parts of Samhain into their own religious practices. They linked this Celtic holiday with their feast of Pomona, the Roman goddess of fruit whose symbol was an apple. In celebration of Pomona the Romans would bob for apples. The Celts adopted this game and added it to their activities on Samhain.

Eventually the Catholic Church replaced these pagan rituals with a day commemorating all Christian saints and martyrs. Thus November 1 was designated as All Saints' Day. In Middle English this was pronounced as *Alholow* or All-hallows which meant all saints. The day before this feast continued to be celebrated by the people of Europe as All-hallows Eve or, as we know it today, Halloween.

These Celtic myths and religious practices were protected and propagated by the spiritual and intellectual leaders known as the Druids. We'll now examine the Druidic Order in detail and discuss how these Celtic priests fared during the Christianization of Ireland.

Chapter 4: Druids

The importance of Druids in Celt society cannot be overstated. They acted as priests, scholars, teachers, physicians, and magistrates. Celtic mythology and religion were taught and preserved by them alone. No sacrifice, whether public or private, could be performed without their supervision. They were the sole interpreters of omens and dreams. All legal issues—from murder to inheritance rights—were adjudged by the Druids. Failure to abide by their judgments meant excommunication from the Celtic community.

According to Caesar, the Druidic Order originated in Britain before spreading to Gaul and parts of Western Europe. By the middle of the first century BC Druids from the continent still traveled to Britain to advance their training and knowledge. Druidic training lasted up to twenty years and involved the study of nearly every aspect of life known to the Celts. Aspiring Druids studied theology, astronomy, geography, history, and natural science.

Although Caesar tells us that the Druids knew the Greek alphabet, the use of writing or note taking was strictly prohibited amongst them. All doctrines and teachings had to be learned by heart. This prohibition against writing had two justifications. First, the Druids believed that writing down their teachings would weaken the memories of their members. Next they feared that the wide-spread publication of their doctrines would lessen their power and prestige in the Celtic world.

Even though we have no written records from the Druids themselves, many of their contemporaries took note of their rituals and beliefs. Several of these writers report the Druids' fondness of mistletoe and their use of the plant during ceremonies. The following quote is from Pliny the Elder (23 to 79 AD):

I can't forget to mention the admiration the Gauls have for mistletoe. The Druids...hold nothing more sacred than this plant and the tree on which it grows—as if it grew only on oaks. They worship only in oak groves and will perform no sacred rites unless a branch of that tree is present. It seems the Druids even get their name from drus (the Greek word for oak). And indeed they think that anything which grows on an oak tree is sent from above and is a sign that the tree was selected by the god himself...In their language they call mistletoe a name meaning "all-healing". They hold sacrifices and sacred meals under oak trees, first leading forward two white bulls with horns bound for the first time. A priest dressed in white then climbs the tree and cuts the mistletoe with a golden sickle, with the plant dropping onto a white cloak. They then sacrifice the bulls while praying that the god will favorably grant his own gift to those to whom he has given it. They believe a drink made with mistletoe will restore fertility to barren livestock and act as a remedy to all poisons. Such is the devotion to frivolous affairs shown by many peoples.[22]

The Celts showed reverence for mistletoe even in the midst of battle. Celtic warriors who found themselves under mistletoe called a momentary truce and refrained from fighting one another until the following day. Today we continue a form of this custom by hanging mistletoe at Christmas and giving affection to family and friends when we're under the plant.

At the top of the Druidic priesthood was an Archdruid invested with supreme authority. This position was held until death and then passed to the next most-eminent Druid. If there was any question regarding who was next in line for the office, the Druids would hold a vote. If this failed to resolve the question, the dispute would be settled by the competing candidates through combat.

The Roman Empire feared the Druids because of their ability to unite the warring Celtic tribes. According to Diodorus, "It has often happened that just as two armies approached each other with swords drawn and spears ready, the Druids will step between the two sides and stop the fighting, as if they had cast a spell on wild beasts."[23]

The will of the Druids even overruled that of the tribal chiefs. Dio Chrysostom (c. 40-111 AD) tells us that "the Celtic kings were not permitted to adopt or plan any course, so that in fact it was these Druids who ruled and the kings became their subordinates and instruments of their judgment."[24]

The Romans also abhorred many of the Druids' religious rituals—most of all the practice of human sacrifice. There are numerous accounts, in both ancient writings and archeological findings, of human sacrifices amongst the Celts. Typically criminals and prisoners of war were used in these sacrifices. Victims were killed in a number of ways. There are records of victims being stabbed, strangled, impaled, or burned to death.

Caesar tells us that in Gaul the Celts built an enormous wooden man (a "wicker man") and filled it with criminals. The structure and all those inside it were then set on fire as part of a ritual sacrifice.

In Kildare County, where Saint Brigid's church would later be established, archeologists have found the ancient remains of a woman who was buried alive in what appears to be a pagan ceremony.

Like many ancient people, the Celts thought that human sacrifices were necessary to appease their gods. They also believed that the Druids could interpret the future by observing a victim's death— how he fell to the ground, how his limbs convulsed, how his blood splattered, etc.

Ancient Romans were violent people who enjoyed watching gladiators maim and kill each other in public stadiums. But the idea of sacrificing a human being in the name of religion disgusted them. Roman citizens were banned from participating in Druidic ceremonies by the Emperor Augustus.

His successor, Tiberius, passed a decree in the senate outlawing Druidry throughout the continent. Finally, Emperor Claudius used the force of the Roman legions to abolish the Druidic Order in Gaul and most of Britain.

The Druids' last stand against the Roman army occurred in 60 AD on the island of Anglesey off the coast of Wales. The battle is vividly described in a famous passage from Tactitus:

The enemy lined the shore in a dense armed mass. Among them were black-robed women with disheveled hair like Furies, brandishing torches. Close by stood Druids, raising their hands to heaven and screaming dreadful curses. The weird spectacle awed the Roman soldiers into a sort of paralysis. They stood still and presented themselves as a target. But then they urged each other (and were urged by the general) not to fear a horde of fanatical women. Onward pressed their standards and they bore down their opponents, enveloping them in the flames of their own torches.[25]

After this crushing defeat the Druids were left with no choice but to abandon Roman Britain and seek refuge in Ireland. The influence of the Druids began to diminish as Christianity spread on the island. During Saint Brigid's lifetime, Druids and Catholic priests would have coexisted in Ireland. In fact, the High King of Ireland, Diarmaid mac Cearrbheoil (544 to 565 AD), had both priests and Druids in his court and took advice from both groups equally.

While Catholic and Druidic priests certainly held conflicting religious beliefs, their roles within the community were quite similar. Both led religious ceremonies, educated the young, cared for the ill, advised kings, and acted as intermediaries between the people and their gods or God. Such similarities would have facilitated the conversion of many Druidic priests to the Catholic faith.

Part 2: The Early Irish Church

Sometime in the seventh century an Irish monk named Muirchu wrote a history of Ireland's conversion to Catholicism. In his history Muirchu tells the story of "a certain great king, a fierce and heathen High King of barbarians." The man's name was Loiguire, the king of Tara and the supreme chieftain of Ireland.

Now Loiguire had about him wise men and magicians and augurs and enchanters and inventors of every evil art, who through their heathenish and idolatrous religion had skill to know and foresee all things before they came to pass. And of these there were two who were preferred beyond the others...And these two by their magical arts frequently foretold the coming of a certain foreign religion, in the manner of a kingdom, with a certain strange and harmful doctrine, brought from a long distance across the seas, proclaimed by a few, accepted by the many, and honored by all; one that would overturn kingdoms, slay kings that resist it, lead away multitudes, destroy all their gods, and, having cast down all the resources of their art, reign forever and ever.[26]

This "foreign religion" that the soothsayers warned of was, of course, Christianity.

The Catholic Church was built on the framework of the Roman Empire. After the Emperor Constantine embraced Christianity in the early fourth century, the religion spread rapidly in the upper classes of Europe. From there it worked its way down to the middle and lower classes of society.

The Church organized and governed itself according to the Roman administrative system. Small villages had a church and a priest. These local churches and priests were part of a larger Catholic community known as a diocese. Each diocese was headed by a bishop and these bishops, in turn, reported to an archbishop in a large city. Above this entire religious network was the Pope in Rome.

Ireland, however, was never part of the Roman Empire and it lacked the

Roman-style political and social structures used by the Church to disseminate Catholicism in continental Europe. Nevertheless, sometime in the early fifth century, about 20 years before the birth of Saint Brigid, Christian missionaries arrived in Ireland and began preaching and proselytizing with great success.

Pope Celestine sent the first bishop to Ireland in 431 AD. The man chosen for this difficult job was a deacon from Gaul named Palladius. According to early church chronicles, Palladius had distinguished himself by combating what was known as the "Pelagian heresy" in Britain.

The teachings of Pelagius denied the idea of original sin. Adherents of the "heresy" believed that God made men free to choose between good and evil and that there was nothing innately sinful about human nature. These teachings conflicted with Church doctrine which held that men could not attain righteousness through their own actions; they needed to seek grace through God alone.

The record of Palladius' mission to Ireland comes from a chronicler named Prosper of Aquitaine. According to Prosper, "Palladius was ordained by Pope Celestine and sent to the Irish believers in Christ as their first bishop."[27] This passage indicates that some of the Irish had embraced Christianity by the early 400s AD. The religion would have been introduced to the island through trade with the Roman Empire as well as by slaves who had been brought to Ireland from Britain and Western Europe. In fact, it is unlikely that Pope Celestine would send a bishop to Ireland unless there was already a sizeable number of Christians on the island who expressly asked the Pope for a religious leader.

Little is known about Palladius or his mission. Most accounts say that he failed miserably before abandoning Ireland and fleeing to Scotland where he died in obscurity.

Muirchu tells us that God Himself thwarted Palladius' mission.

But God prohibited him; because no one can receive anything from earth unless it were given to him from heaven;

neither did those wild and rough people readily receive his teaching, nor did he himself desire to spend a long time in a land not his own...Palladius crossed the sea and died in the country of the Britons.[28]

But these stories are likely exaggerated or completely fabricated in order to make his successor, Saint Patrick, look more impressive. It's even possible that Palladius had some success in his early missionary work. His accomplishments, however, may have been attributed to Patrick by later Church writers.

Chapter 5: Saint Patrick

It's possible that Palladius himself brought Patrick to Ireland as part of his missionary team. At the time Palladius arrived in Ireland, Patrick would have been about thirty years old with a good knowledge of Irish geography, culture, and language-- an ideal candidate for the mission.

We are fortunate to have two documents written by Patrick. The first is a semi-autobiographical work known as the *Confession*. The second is a letter written by Patrick to a warlord named Coroticus. In this letter, Patrick condemns Coroticus for murdering and enslaving Celts that Patrick recently converted to Christianity.

In these writings we get a strong sense of who Patrick was as a person. In many ways he was a humble and somewhat insecure man. He describes himself as rustic and uneducated and he frequently expresses embarrassment for his poor grasp of the Latin language in which he wrote. Yet a much different Patrick is perceived when reading his sharply worded letter to Coroticus. When provoked Patrick became a bold and passionate defender of his faith and its adherents.

Patrick was born on the west coast of Britain sometime in the early 400s. Although his father was a deacon and his grandfather was a priest, Patrick did not have much respect for Christianity in his youth. He tells us "I did not know

God...and did not keep his precepts, nor obey our priests who used to remind us of our salvation."[29] In response to Patrick's contempt for the church, God "brought down his fury" upon him.

One night, when Patrick was sixteen years old, Irish pirates invaded his village, kidnapped him, and sold him into slavery on the west coast of Ireland. He spent six years of his life in slavery working on a pasture.

During those years, Patrick turned to the religion that he had disregarded in his youth.

More and more did the love of God, and my fear of Him increase, and my spirit was moved so that each day I said up to a hundred prayers and up to a hundred more each night. I used to stay out in the forests and on the mountain and I would wake up before daylight to pray in the snow, in icy coldness, in rain, and I felt neither ill nor any slothfulness because the spirit of God was burning within me.[30]

One evening, after fasting and prayer, Patrick heard a voice in his sleep.

(This is one of several dreams mentioned in the *Confession*. Patrick's dreams must have been extremely vivid. He writes of them as being a source of both horror and inspiration.) The voice told Patrick that it was time for him to leave Ireland and return home. He must act immediately because his ship was ready.

As mentioned earlier, Patrick was on the west coast of Ireland and, at the time of his escape, there were no ships on his side of the island that sailed directly to Britain or any other port in Europe. So Patrick, who was then about 21 years old, escaped from servitude and, as a fugitive, walked across the breadth of Ireland until he arrived on its eastern coast. It was an extremely dangerous thing to do. If Patrick had been captured during the journey, the punishment for his actions would have been severe. Patrick tells us that God watched over him during his escape and directed his route until he finally reached a ship that was about to sail for Gaul.

The day I arrived, the ship was about to leave the place. I said I needed to set sail with them, but the captain was not at all pleased. He replied unpleasantly and angrily: "Don't you dare try to come with us." When I heard that, I left them and went back to the hut where I had lodgings. I began to pray while I was going; and before I even finished the prayer, I heard one of them shout aloud at me: "Come quickly – those men are calling you!" I turned back right away, and they began to say to me: "Come – we'll trust you. Prove you're our friend in any way you wish."... This is how I got to go with them, and we set sail right away.[31]

Patrick then adds, "I refused to suck their breasts, because of my reverence for God."[32] Patrick makes this bizarre statement in a matter-of-fact way, as though it was a common initiation among pagan sailors. Although some scholars believe that the statement is being used figuratively, it seems more likely that Patrick was speaking literally and that Celtic mariners sucked the nipples of the other crewmen before joining a ship.

We have no other details of the voyage except that it lasted for three days and that dogs were included as part of the cargo. During this time Irish wolfhounds were highly valued in Europe. They were used primarily to protect dwellings and to hunt game. The hounds were so massive—"each as big as a mule," according to the *Book of Lismore*—that they were even deployed against enemy combatants in war.

There is also a story in the *Book of Lismore* of one of these hounds wandering into Brigid's home when she was a girl. The dog walked into the kitchen where Brigid was preparing bacon for her father and his noble guests. The dog seemed miserable and hungry so Brigid happily fed every last piece of meat to the hound. When her father went to the kitchen to check on the dinner the bacon miraculously reappeared.

A few years after fleeing Ireland, Patrick was once again home with his family in Britain. He tells us that he was "welcomed home as a son" and that his family pleaded with him never to leave again. When we consider what Patrick risked and endured to return home, we can easily assume that he wanted to be there—safe from harm and living as a free man with his loved ones. But again Patrick received a powerful message in his dreams that he could not ignore.

There, in a vision of the night, I saw a man whose name was Victoricus coming from Ireland with innumerable letters, and he gave me one of them. I read the beginning of the letter: 'The Voice of the Irish' and as I was reading I heard the voice of those who were beside the forest of Folcut near the western sea. They were crying as if with one voice: 'We beg you, holy youth, that you shall come and walk among us again.' And I was stung intensely in my heart so that I could read no more, and thus I awoke.[33]

He first traveled to Gaul where he received his religious education and became a member of the clergy, quickly earning the title of bishop. Sometime in the 430s he arrived in Ireland and began his missionary work.

Fifth century Ireland was a wild and dangerous place and many of the Irish would have perceived Patrick as a direct threat to their way of life. He tells us that he "daily expected to be murdered or betrayed or reduced to slavery."[34]   In fact, at one point he was captured, robbed, and confined in chains for two weeks. We're not told exactly who seized him. But eventually he was released and his stolen items were returned to him. Patrick admits that he wished to abandon his mission and return home but he felt "bound by the Spirit" to stay with the Irish and complete his work. He would remain in Ireland for the rest of his life.

Although Patrick described himself in humble terms, he wrote openly about his success in converting Ireland to Catholicism. He tells us that through his work "thousands would be reborn in God" and "clergy would be ordained everywhere."[35]   Such mass conversions were common in the early years of Christianity. In the Book of Acts, for instance, we read that Saint Peter made 3,000 converts after giving just one sermon.[36] (Sadly most priests today could give 3,000 sermons and not get a single convert.) Given the speed at which Christianity spread throughout Europe, it seems these stories of mass conversions are legitimate.

But why was Patrick so successful?

It seems undeniable that he was a passionate advocate for the Church and that he possessed the charisma necessary to command the attention and respect of the unruly Celts.

Patrick preached to both rich and poor. He tells of his work with widows, slaves, and women. Many of them were receptive to the new faith which taught that all were equal in the eyes of God and that those who worshipped Him would ascend to an eternal paradise when they died. The women showed great affection for Patrick and frequently offered him gifts and ornaments as tokens of their appreciation. He mentions one female convert in particular, "a most beautiful, native-born Irish woman of adult age whom I baptized." This was done "without her father's consent and with the enduring persecutions and deceitful hindrances of her parents."[37]

Among the Celtic leaders Patrick used generous gifts and bribes along with his sermons to persuade their conversion. Patrick's payroll included "those who were administering justice in all the regions" and he estimates that he paid to them "not less than the price of fifteen slaves"—a huge sum of money.   If the king of a tribe embraced Christianity, it often meant that the members of the tribe would likewise become Christians. This could result in mass conversions of dozens or even hundreds of the Irish all at once.

Finally, the spread of Christianity in Ireland was largely due to Patrick's tolerance of the native customs and his willingness to incorporate ancient Irish practices with the Catholic rites.

A similar approach was taken by the Church in dealing with the Anglo-Saxons in Britain. Consider, for example, the following quote from Pope Gregory I to his religious leaders in England in the year 601:

The temples of idols in that nation should not be destroyed, but...the idols themselves that are in them should be. Let blessed water be prepared, and sprinkled in these temples, and altars constructed, and relics deposited since, if these same temples are well built, it is needful that they should be transferred from the worship of idols to the service of the true God; that, when the people themselves see that these temples are not destroyed, they may put away error from their heart, and, knowing and adoring the true God, may have recourse with the more familiarity to the places they have been accustomed to.[38]

The Irish responded favorably to this lenient approach. In fact, it's remarkable that the Irish Celts, who were known throughout Europe for their savagery, were Christianized within a few generations without the Church suffering a single martyr.

By the end of Patrick's life, sometime in the late 400s, Catholicism had been established in Ireland, existing alongside the ancient pagan religion. Slowly Irish paganism faded away but many of its aspects merged into Catholicism and a unique form of Celtic Christianity prevailed over the island. It was during this time that Brigid lived her life and made her mark on Ireland and the Catholic Church.

Part 3: Saint Brigid

Chapter 6: Brigid's Birth

The oldest source on Saint Brigid was written around 650 AD (approximately 125 years after her death) by a monk in Kildare named Cogitosus. Because Cogitosus was the writer closest to Brigid in time and location, I have used his work (the *Life of Saint Brigid*) as my primary source of information for our saint. Another source that I relied on heavily is the *Book of Lismore* written sometime in the fifteenth century by scribes in County Cork.

Brigid's father was a chieftain named Dubthach who ruled over a small tribe somewhere in the vicinity of present-day Kildare. Although ancient texts make no mention of Dubthach's religion, he frequently associates himself with both priests and druids and readily accepts advice from either camp. This was a common practice among the Irish ruling class during the fifth and sixth centuries.

One day Dubthach purchased a young female servant named Broisech from a nearby village. Soon thereafter he impregnated the girl. When his wife, Blaithbec, heard the news she was enraged. She demanded that Dubthach take Broisech far away from their land and sell her. If he refused, his wife would divorce him and take back her dowry. Dubthach, although fond of Broisech, reluctantly complied with his wife's orders.

Accordingly, Dubthach put Broisech into his chariot and proceeded to escort her from his land. Along the way the chariot passed the home of a druid named Maithgen. Upon hearing the wheels of the chariot rattling on the road, Maithgen knew instantly that it was the local chief and he rushed outside to meet with Dubthach. He asked if Broicsech was pregnant and Dubthach affirmed that she was carrying his child.

Then, through his powers of prophecy, Maithgen told the couple that they will have a daughter and she will be "conspicuous, radiant, and will shine like a sun among the stars of heaven."[39]

This prophecy greatly affected Dubthach who had only sons (six of them) and he was thrilled to have a daughter. Not just any daughter—his child would shine brighter than any other in the land. At once he determined to return home with Broisech even if it meant losing his wife and the dowry that came with her.

Despite her threats, Dubthach's wife remained with him and all three lived together in the same dwelling. To understand this unusual situation, some knowledge of ancient Irish law is necessary. Although Broisech was originally Dubthach's servant (i.e., his property), she would have acquired some rights upon conceiving his child. In many cases a woman in Broisech's situation would be treated as a secondary wife to the child's father. Moreover, the child would have the same status as any of the man's other children.

Shortly after returning home, Dubthach was visited by two Bishops from Scotland. They were Bishop Mel, who would later become one of Brigid's closest friends, and his associate Bishop Melchu. Somehow the prophecy made by the druid Maithgen had reached them and they traveled to Ireland to bless both the unborn child and her mother.

During the meeting with the bishops, Blaithbec expressed her anger and jealousy over Broisech and the affection and favoritism that Dubthach showed towards the young woman. After seeing her displeasure, Bishop Mel tells Blaithbec that the unborn child will one day be of great help to her. Blaithbec herself was pregnant at this time with Dubthach's seventh son. The other six boys were already seen by the bishop as being ill tempered and knavish. He prophesied that the seventh son would be the worst of them all. But if these boys followed the ways of their sister they would be redeemed. As for Blaithbec herself, there would be no redemption. According to Bishop Mel, she would be forever cursed because of her treatment of Broisech.

While the bishop was making these predictions, a bard arrived at Dubthach's home. It is unclear what brought the bard to the house but he immediately noted the strife that Broisech was causing and offered to buy her from Dubthach. Despite his fondness for Broisech and their unborn child, Dubthach agreed to sell them to the bard. However, Bishop Mel pleaded with Dubthach to sell only Broicsech while keeping the rights to his unborn child. Both Dubthach and the bard agreed to these terms and Broicsech was handed over to the bard that evening.

The bard soon sold the young woman to a druid who would keep her as his servant for many years thereafter.

We are not given many details about this druid except that he was originally from Tyrconnell in Northern Ireland. We can also infer from the texts that he had some standing within his community due to the fact that he associated himself with tribal rulers and had the means to own multiple servants including Broisech.

One night this druid prepared a great feast and invited the King of Conaille to join him. The guests at the party were being entertained by a soothsayer. The king's pregnant wife was in attendance and one of the guests asked the soothsayer when the queen would have her child.

Rather than responding to the question, the soothsayer turned to Broisech and told her that she would give birth at sunrise—neither within nor without the house and that the child born to her "shall surpass every other child in Ireland."[40]

The next morning at sunrise, in accordance with the prophecy, Broisech gave birth in the doorway of her home while she was carrying a vessel of milk into or out of the house. We're told that this birth took place on a Wednesday on the eighth moon of the lunar calendar. It was February first. The precise year is unknown but most texts agree that the birth took place in the middle of the fifth century.

After the child was born, other servants who lived with the druid aided Broisech and washed the newborn with the milk from the vessel. It's unclear why this was done. Perhaps it's symbolic of the child's future role as the saint of dairymaids. Regardless of its symbolism, the practice of cleaning newborns with milk was carried on in Ireland for many years thereafter.

Chapter 7:
Brigid's Name

The infant needed a name, of course, and this name would come to the druid one night in his sleep. We're told that as the druid slept he was visited by three angels dressed in white. In his dream the angels baptized the child with oil. When they were done, one of them turned to the druid and said that the girl's name shall be Brigid.

As mentioned earlier, the name Brigid derives from the pagan goddess Brigantia who was worshipped throughout the Celtic world. Almost every western European country has some form of the name. In France it is "Brigitte" or "Brigette". In Germany and Scandinavia they use "Bridget". The Italian version of the name is "Brigida" or "Brigitta". The name Brigid was used frequently by the Irish in honor of their saint up to the twentieth century. In fact, prior to the 1900s, almost every Irish household had a daughter named Brigid.

The name fell out of use for a couple reasons.

First, as hostility grew between the Irish and English, the English derisively referred to all Irish girls as "Biddies". Because "Biddy" was the nickname for Brigid, Irish women became less inclined to give the name to their daughters.

Second, a great deal of uncertainty and confusion about the name's spelling and pronunciation arose in the late 1800s. During that time German manufacturers produced many of the religious statues and objects of worship sold to Catholics in Ireland and America. These manufacturers—due to ignorance or apathy—often marketed and distributed items that were supposed to represent Saint Brigid of Ireland but in fact bore the name and image of Saint Bridget, a Swedish saint from the 1300s. Consequently, many families in Ireland and America mistakenly gave their daughters the name of this Swedish saint.

To make matters worse, the Swedish pronunciation was often applied to the Irish spelling of the name. Originally the name Brigid would be pronounced "Brigg-id". As the Swedish version of the name came into use, so did it's pronunciation. This meant that the "g" sound was changed to a "j" producing a pronunciation of "Brid-jid".

Chapter 8:
Brigid's Youth

After Brigid's birth, the druid moved his household some distance from Kildare. Where he relocated to is unclear. Cogitosus claims that Brigid was moved to the home of Broisech's mother in Connaught. The *Book of Lismore*, however, states that the druid "went to his own patrimony."[41] This means that the druid returned to his family's estate which is alluded to as being in Tyrconnell in Ulster. Regardless of where baby Brigid was brought, we can assume from these sources that it was far from her father's residence due to the fact that all correspondence with him had to be done through messengers.

We're told that as an infant Brigid refused any nourishment given to her by the druid. As a pagan any sustenance that he provided was considered impure or unclean. Instead the only food that Brigid could consume was milk from a white cow with red ears. The cow was tended by a faithful Christian woman who was in the druid's service.

In this story we see a mixing or muddling of pagan and Christian beliefs that is common throughout the tales of Saint Brigid. On one hand, the white cow with red ears would be considered sacred to the pagan Celts. To them the color white represented purity and sanctity while the color red was identified with the Otherworld. On the other hand, the idea of food or drink being unclean because it was prepared or served by a pagan was a Christian notion. The Irish scribes relating this story combine the two incongruent concepts in their effort to make Brigid seem especially venerable.

There are just two more stories about Brigid's infancy. The first says that one day Brigid's mother put her down for a nap and then went outside to care for the cows. Suddenly the house was engulfed in a fire that rose from the earth to heaven. Neighbors rushed to the house to save the child. But when they got there the flames had disappeared. Those who saw the spectacle attributed the flame to baby Brigid's grace and holiness.

In a much less dramatic tale, Broisech and the druid were in a field with Brigid when a pile of cow dung inexplicably caught fire. When the couple moved closer to observe what had happened the fire instantly went out.

These tales, odd as they may seem, were written to show Brigid's connection, even in her infancy, with fire. As we'll discuss later, Brigid and her followers at Kildare tended a perpetual fire, a pagan ritual that was carried on for centuries in Christian Ireland.

Little is said about Brigid's childhood except that she took great care of the animals on her estate and that she helped the poor in her community. These would be common themes throughout her life.

According to the *Book of Lismore*, "when boldness and strength and size came to Brigid she desired to go and visit her fatherland."[42] A similar line appears in Cogitosus's narrative. However, neither source tells us how old Brigid is when she asked to return home to her father. Nevertheless, we are told that she was still in the care of a nurse at this time. So it's likely that she had not reached adolescence.

According to her wishes the druid immediately sent to Dubthach informing him of Brigid's miracles and of her desire to return home. Dubthach was overjoyed by the news and came at once to retrieve his daughter.

Pursuant to the agreement made before Brigid's birth, she was freely returned to her father while her mother, Broisech, remained the property of the druid. We don't know how Brigid felt about leaving her mother behind. But it's likely that Brigid missed her and harbored some resentment over the situation. As we'll discuss, years later Brigid returned to the druid and boldly demanded her mother's release.

The relationship between Brigid and her father was contentious. Dubthach seemed to be a caring man. He had a great deal of authority over the women in his life (his wife, his daughter, and Broisech); yet he was not a dictator and it seems as though he wanted to make everyone happy. He was excited when he first learned that he was having a daughter and he was happy when she returned home to him. But young Brigid's behavior quickly caused Dubthach to lose his patience.

After returning home to Dubthach's estate, Brigid began giving away her father's wealth to almost anyone that needed it. She let thieves run off with his pigs. She fed his bacon to a stray hound. She gave his cattle to the poor. Any possessions she found were handed out to the less fortunate. This enraged Dubthach and he finally decided to sell her into bondage. He put her in his chariot and brought her to the King of Leinster. Brigid was ordered to wait outside while Dubthach went into the King's home to make his offer. The king was surprised by the proposition.

"Wherefore sellest thou thine own daughter?" he asked.

"Not hard to say" responded Dubthach. "She is selling my wealth and bestowing it on wretched worthless men!"[43]

Outside, while this discussion was taking place, a leper wandered past Brigid who was still seated in her father's chariot. Next to her was Dubthach's sword, a valuable item for any Irish chieftain. Without any consideration to the situation she was in, Brigid took the sword and gave it to the leper.

When Dubthach came to retrieve Brigid, he was infuriated to see his sword missing. He angrily pushed her in front of the king who asked why she would give away her father's wealth in such a way. Brigid responded that she would give away all of her father's possessions and the king's possessions too if they were at her disposal.

Upon hearing this the king decided that he did not want this troublesome girl in his service. But he was impressed by her charity and her concern for others. Turning to Dubthach he said "it is not meant for us to deal with this maiden, for her merit before God is higher than ours."[44]

Brigid would again butt heads with Dubthach over her mother. When Brigid received news that her mother was sick, she asked Dubthach for permission to visit her. He refused and Brigid went anyway.

Brigid arrived at the druid's estate where she found her mother worn down by work and physically ill. Out of compassion, Brigid went to work performing her mother's chores. These chores included tending the cows and churning butter. In her customary way, Brigid began handing out the druid's butter to the poor people living nearby. A herdsman on the druid's estate confronted Brigid and demanded to know why she was giving away the butter. Brigid responded, "In Christ's name it is that I feed the poor for He is in the person of every faithful poor man."[45]

Word of Brigid's actions reached the druid who came to Brigid and demanded an explanation. Ignoring the druid's demands Brigid looked up to the sky and prayed to the "Prince of the World" asking for abundance on the druid's estate. This prayer was immediately answered. Baskets were filled with butter and the druid's livestock became fatter and healthier than ever. Stunned by the miracle, the druid offered it all to Brigid. "Take thou your cows" said Brigid, "but give me my mother's freedom."[46] The druid readily freed Broisech and, at the same time, converted to Christianity and pledged to follow Brigid for the rest of his life.

Brigid and her mother then returned home to Dubthach. There is no mention of Dubthach's reaction to the return of Broisech. We know that he was fond of her before being forced to sell her into slavery. So perhaps he was pleased with her return. However, he did forbid Brigid from visiting her and it is possible that Broisech's reappearance in Dubthach's life caused additional tension and stress for the man—especially if his wife were still alive. Unfortunately we aren't given any of these details.

Brigid's final act of defiance was in refusing to marry a noble man her father and brothers had chosen for her. One of her brothers, a young man named Beccan, taunted Brigid by saying a girl with eyes as fair as hers must rest her head on a pillow next to a husband. Upon hearing this Brigid glared at her brother and said "Lo, here for thee is thy delightful eye, O Beccan!"[47] She wedged her finger into the socket and plucked out her eye. The eye dangled on her cheek. Her father and brothers were horrified. They assured her that she would not have to marry anyone against her will. Brigid then calmly pushed the eye back into place without any damage being done. After this Dubthach urged his daughter to join the church.

"O daughter, says he, put a veil on thy head. If thou hast dedicated thy virginity to God, I will not snatch it from Him. Deo gratias, says Brigid."[48]

Chapter 9: Brigid's Ordination

Brigid was probably in her late teens when she was ordained. We're told that "on the eighteenth she took the veil"[49] though it's unclear whether this is the eighteenth day of the month or the eighteenth year of Brigid's life. She was joined by seven other young women. Brigid sought out Bishop Mel, the same bishop who visited her father prior to her birth, to perform the ceremony. The young women first encountered a pupil of the bishop named MacCaill. He told them that to reach the bishop they would need to travel a "trackless roads with marshes, deserts and pools."[50] Undeterred by such a difficult trek, Brigid and her companions eventually found Bishop Mel and he readily agreed to perform the ordination at the altar of his church.

During the ceremony "through the Grace of God" Bishop Mel was compelled to ordain Brigid as a bishop. As he was performing this ceremony MacCaill stopped him and protested that the order of a bishop cannot be conferred on a woman. "No power have I in this matter" answered Bishop Mel, "God hath given unto her this honor."[51]

It's questionable whether Brigid was in fact a bishop. The early Irish church was certainly more liberal than its counterparts on the continent when it came to ordaining bishops and bishops in Ireland were also quite numerous in Brigid's time. So it is plausible that a woman could be ordained as a bishop. However, Cogitosus tells us that Brigid was unable to perform baptisms and that she needed a male priest to accompany her wherever she went in order to handle such matters. Thus the case can be made that Brigid did not have all the power and authority that was bestowed on a male member of the clergy.

We can glean from the story of Brigid's ordination that she had a high regard for Bishop Mel. In fact, aside from Saint Brigid herself, Bishop Mel is mentioned more than anyone in the texts.

He was a bishop in Scotland before traveling to Ireland, although it's unclear exactly where he was born, raised, and educated. At the time Brigid took the veil, he must have been at least middle aged and apparently living in a secluded area of the island. After ordaining Brigid, he would be by her side for the rest of his life. He acted as Brigid's advisor and protector. He was almost certainly her close friend.

Brigid, for her own part, made sure Mel was well provided for and that he received just compensation for his work. Often his payment came in the form of cattle and ale. Nevertheless, he was not spared from Brigid's occasional bouts of anger. For instance, she once scolded Bishop Mel for his "disobedience" when a cart he was driving tipped over and sent Brigid tumbling to the ground.

Up to the ordination of Brigid, the stories have an easy-to-follow chronology. Brigid is conceived. She's born. She goes through her childhood and adolescence. Finally, she joins the church and begins her ministry. Unfortunately, there is almost no chronological order to the series of events that happen between her ordination and her death—a period of approximately 75 years. Consequently, the following chapters will not be based on any type of timeline. Instead each chapter will focus on a particular topic or theme that is important in the tales of Saint Brigid.

Chapter 10:
Brigid's Character

The *Book of Lismore* gives the following description of Brigid's character:

Now there never hath been anyone more bashful or more modest or more gentle or more humble or sager or more harmonious than Brigid. She never washed her hands or her feet or her head among men. She never looked at the face of a man. She never would speak without blushing. She was abstinent. She was innocent. She was prayerful. She was patient. She was glad in God's commandments. She was firm. She was humble. She was forgiving. She was loving. She was a consecrated casket for keeping Christ's body and blood. She was a temple of God.[52]

Saint Brigid was undoubtedly generous and compassionate towards the sick and the poor and she certainly lived a life of devotion and abstinence. The chapters below describing her charity and miracles will attest to that. But we would be mistaken if we thought of Brigid as a timid or blushing woman who "never looked at the face of a man."

As we've already seen and as we'll continue to observe, Brigid did not shy away from conflict and she certainly did not give deference to the men in her life. She argued with her father, her brothers, the druid who raised her, and Bishop Mel. As her prominence grew, she even spoke boldly to the King of Leinster himself on several occasions.

When Brigid was disobeyed, she often became quite cruel. Here are just a few examples:

- A woman once brought a basket of apples to Brigid. Brigid told the woman to give the apples to some lepers who were standing nearby. The woman protested; the apples were for Brigid, not the lepers. Annoyed by the woman's refusal, Brigid cursed her apple orchard. From that day forward the woman's land was barren and not a single apple grew from its trees.

- As mentioned earlier, Brigid was taunted by one of her brother's (Beccan) when she refused to marry a nobleman her family had picked for her. Brigid removed her eye in protest of the marriage. When the marriage was called off, Brigid replaced her eye and then cursed Beccan by blinding him for the rest of his life.

- Two lepers came to Brigid asking to be healed. She told one to wash the other. The leper who had been washed was cured. Brigid then asked the man who had been healed to wash his companion so that he too could be cured. The healthy man refused out of fear of contracting the disease again. For his insolence, Brigid cursed him with leprosy and he remained ill from that day on.

The extreme nature of Brigid's personality—one day charitable and generous, the next day cruel and unforgiving—is noticeable in almost all her stories.

Chapter 11: Brigid's Friends and Followers

Brigid spent most of her life surrounded by friends and followers. Below is a summary of just some of the people who were involved in Brigid's life and her church at Kildare.

Conleth the Hermit

Besides Bishop Mel, probably the most significant person in Brigid's monastic life was a hermit named Conleth. Upon establishing her church at Kildare, Brigid sought out Conleth who was living in the wilderness of Ireland in solitude. She wanted Conleth to serve as bishop and govern the operations at her new church. Conleth agreed and soon the church at Kildare "grew like a vine with its roots in Ireland."[53]

Not much detail is given about this important man. We're told that before meeting Brigid, he was already famous throughout Ireland for his miracles. He was also an artist and craftsman and it's likely that he contributed to some of the manuscripts and works of art that the Church of Kildare was producing at the time.

The stories concerning Brigid and Conleth shed some light on how Brigid administered her church and dealt with those who were part of the ministry at Kildare. For instance, we're told that one day Conleth acquired religious vestments from "overseas seas," most likely from France or Rome.

Although Conleth was a former hermit who ostensibly cared little for worldly goods, he was very enamored by these vestments and looked forward to showing them off at the next mass. Unfortunately, he left them unguarded at the church and they fell into the hands of Brigid who promptly handed them off to the poor. We don't hear of Conleth's reaction to having his valuable vestments given away, although we can imagine that he felt at least some indignation.

Conleth's bad luck continued when he asked Brigid for permission to visit Rome. Throughout the stories of Saint

Brigid, many of those in her religious community showed a great interest in Rome and a strong desire to travel there. According to author Thomas Olden:

> *Rome, the capital of the world, must have exercised a powerful attraction on the races on the outskirts of the Empire. Apart from its ancient glory, it was now sanctified in their eyes as the burial-place, according to popular belief, of the Apostles Peter and Paul...Among so religious and inquisitive a people as the Irish, there must have been an eager desire to visit the great city, but it was the policy of the Irish Church...to throw obstacles in the way of this intercourse, and to preserve the native institutions from foreign influence.[54]*

Indeed, Brigid flat out rejected Conleth's request. Ignoring Brigid's orders, Conleth packed his bags and set out for Rome. Before he left, Brigid warned him that he would neither reach Rome nor return home again. According to her prophecy, Conleth was attacked and devoured by wolves before he left the Irish shore.

Ninnid the Scholar

This scholar ran past Brigid one day as she was feeding her sheep. Whether they knew each other beforehand is unclear. Brigid demanded "What art thou doing, O Sage...and whither art thou wending so quickly?"[55] Ninnid tells Brigid that he is going to heaven and that she should not delay him unless she intends to make his journey there a happy one. Perhaps Ninnid was joking when he told Brigid that he was running toward heaven. Maybe he was speaking metaphysically. Either way, Brigid asked him to hold her hand and recite an Our Father. Ninnid agreed and after their encounter they remained friends for the rest of their lives.

We're told that Ninnid never again washed the hand that Brigid held when they prayed. Thus he acquired the nickname "Ninnid of the Pure Hand".

He traveled to Rome after befriending Brigid and at some point became a member of the clergy. We don't know how long he stayed in Rome but he returned to Ireland to be at Brigid's bedside when she died. She received commune from Ninnid before he read her last rites and "sent her spirit thereafter to heaven."[56]

King of Leinster

The king first met Brigid when her father offered her for sale. We know that the king was impressed by Brigid and it seems that his admiration for her continued throughout their lives. The king attended Brigid's church and listened to her preaching. For her part, Brigid made ale for the king and spent a great deal of time at his court. Most stories about Brigid and the king involve negotiations between the two. Typically Brigid is beseeching the king to have lenience and mercy on his poorer subjects.

Probably the most famous and most amusing of these stories is the tale about the woodman who killed the king's pet fox. The fox was trained to perform several tricks that greatly entertained the king and his entourage. For some reason this fox wandered past the woodman who believed the animal was wild and a threat to the village. The woodman killed the fox.

This enraged the king. He sentenced the woodman to death and ordered that his family be sold into slavery unless a new fox capable of all the same tricks was brought to him at once.

Hearing of this sentence, Brigid leaped into her chariot and raced towards the king's palace hoping to dissuade him. Along the way she prayed fervently to God for help. As she prayed a wild fox came running out of the woods and jumped into her lap. Brigid and her fox appeared before the king and the fox performed all of the tricks that the old fox knew. This prompted "tumultuous applause" from the king and his court. The woodsman and his family were set free and Brigid returned to her monastery.

Afterwards the fox scattered out of the king's court and ran back into the woods. The king, his hounds, and a large search party went out to recover the fox but it was never seen again.

On another occasion the king lent a sword to Brigid's father who liked the weapon very much. Dubthach did not want to give the sword back. So he sent

Brigid to the king hoping that she could convince him to let Dubthach keep it.

Along the way she met one of the king's servants. The man pleaded with Brigid to free him from his bondage. He promised that if she obtained his freedom he would convert to Christianity and become one of her followers.

After listening to this man Brigid confronted the king and demanded both the sword for her father and freedom for the king's servant. The king scoffed and asked Brigid why he should be so generous. She responded that in return she would grant health to the king's children and eternal life in heaven to the king himself when he died. The king rejected this offer. He was unconcerned about the health of his children and as for the promise of heaven, the king replied "I see it not, therefore I ask it not."[57] Instead what the King of Leinster wanted more than anything was a long life and victory in battle. Brigid agreed to grant these things to him in exchange for what she desired. The deal was done and we're told that after that day the king went on to win thirty battles in Ireland and nine in Scotland.

Saint Patrick

It's questionable whether Patrick and Brigid knew one another. Patrick probably died in the late 400s. Brigid was born about fifty years earlier but we don't have exact dates for either event. If Patrick and Brigid were active in the Irish church at the same time, they were probably acquainted and there could be some truth to the tales of these two patron saints.

The most interesting story concerning them takes place at a synod in the town of Teltown in the province of Leinster where Patrick resided according to the texts.

The clergy in that region met to hear accusations being made by a local woman against one of Patrick's associates, a man named Bishop Bron. The woman, whose name is not given, appeared before the synod holding a baby boy. According to the woman she conceived the child through an illicit relationship with Bishop Bron.

After the woman spoke, Brigid stepped forward and implored the woman not to speak falsely. The woman stared at Brigid with indignation and began to repeat her allegations. Suddenly the woman's tongue swelled up in her mouth and she was unable to speak.

Brigid then turned to the small child, made the sign of the cross over his mouth and asked "Who is thy father?". To the crowd's amazement the boy looked at Brigid and said "My father is a wretched man who lives on the outskirts of the assembly."[58] Through this miracle Bishop Bron and his reputation were saved.

Chapter 12: Kildare Church

Saint Brigid's greatest achievement was almost certainly the establishment of her church in Kildare. The location, we're told, was chosen by Brigid and Bishop Mel. It was probably a site for pagan rituals in former times. The name Kildare derives from *Cill Dara* which translates to "church of the oak tree."

As Brigid and Bishop Mel were reviewing land for the church, a train of the king's horses rode past. These horses pulled carts loaded with posts, wattle, and other building supplies. Two of Brigid's maidens approached the man directing the procession. They asked him if he could spare some of the materials he was transporting so that they could construct a church. The man scoffed at the girls, refused their request, and told them to move out of his way. Instantly the entire chain of horses was struck down to the ground and paralyzed by an invisible force. The king, who was present, was shocked by the sight and he rushed forward to speak with Brigid. He told her that the land and all of the building materials would be hers if she revived his horses. This was done and the king ordered his men to immediately begin construction on Brigid's church.

Cogitosus gives us a detailed description of what was built:

The church is spacious in its floor area, and it rises to an extreme height. It is adorned with painted boards and has on the inside three wide chapels, all under the roof of the large building and separated by wooden partitions....The church has many windows and an ornamented door on the right side through which the priests and the faithful of the male sex enter the building. There is another door on the left through which the virgins and the congregation of the female faithful are accustomed to enter. And so, in one great basilica, a large number of people, arranged by rank and sex, in orderly division separated by partitions, offers prayers with a single spirit to the almighty Lord.[59]

The church was founded in the late 400s. By the time of Cogitosus in the late 700s, Kildare was a busy ecclesiastical center. He writes:

But who could convey in words the supreme beauty of her church and the countless wonders of her city, of which we would speak? "City" is the right word for it: that so many people are living there justifies the title. It is a great metropolis, within whose outskirts— which Saint Brigid marked out with a clearly defined boundary—no earthly adversary is feared, nor any incursion of enemies. For the city is the safest place of refuge among all the towns of the whole land of the Irish, with all their fugitives. It is a place where the treasures of kings are looked after, and it is reckoned to be supreme in good order. And who could number the varied crowds and countless people who gather in from all territories? Some come for the abundance of festivals; others come to watch the crowds go by; others come with great gifts to the celebration of the birth into heaven of Saint Brigid.[60]

A number of religious attractions could be found in Kildare at the time Cogitosus was writing. As discussed earlier, the *Book of Kildare* was created and housed at the monastery. The remains of Saint Brigid and Conleth were also enshrined within the church. Finally, the church maintained a perpetual fire which burned from Brigid's time until 1220 when Bishop Henry of Dublin ordered it extinguished. This was done as part of the Church's effort to eliminate the pagan symbolism that still prevailed in Ireland. The Church's prohibition included the veneration of wells, springs, and stones. Nevertheless, the Irish stubbornly clung to these traditions and Saint Brigid's fire was soon re-lit. It burned until the sixteenth century when it was permanently doused pursuit to the orders of Archbishop George Browne.

Gerald of Wales, who visited the monastery in the late 1100s, refers to Brigid's fire as "the first of all miracles" found at Kildare. He tells us that the flame was originally tended by Saint Brigid and 19 of her maidens. From the time the church was founded until his visit hundreds of years later, the fire burned continuously and it was still in the care of 20 nuns. Each night one of these women would be responsible for watching over the fire, supplying it with wood, and using a bellow to sustain the flames. No one was allowed to blow on the fire. Men were strictly forbidden from approaching the flame or its guardians. A circular hedge surrounded the area where the fire burned and it was not to be crossed.

According to Gerald this rule was violated at least twice. One man put his foot over the hedge with the intent to enter the sacred area. His companions restrained him before he could go any further but it was too late. The foot that crossed the hedge instantly withered and soon fell off the man's leg. On another occasion a man managed to cross the hedge and blow on the fire. Divine vengeance struck him and he soon became mad and died shortly thereafter. Gerald relates the story as follows:

At Kildare an archer of the household of Earl Richard crossed over the hedge and blew upon Brigid's fire. He jumped back immediately and went mad. Whomsoever he met, he blew upon his face and said: "See! That is how I blew on Brigid's fire." And so he ran through all the houses of the whole settlement, and wherever he saw a fire he blew upon it using the same words. Eventually he was caught and bound by his companions, but asked to be brought to the nearest water. As soon as he was brought there, his mouth was so parched that he drank so much that, while still in their hands he burst in the middle and died.[61]

The original church was remodeled and rebuilt a number of times due to aging and occasional disasters. It finally fell into disrepair after the English Reformation in the sixteenth century and was completely ruined in the following century during the Irish Confederate Wars.

In 1875 restoration work began by the English architect George Edmund Street. The restoration was completed in 1896 and today it is one of two cathedrals in the United Dioceses of Meath and Kildare.

Chapter 13: Brigid's Miracles

Almost every story in the life of Saint Brigid involves some type of miracle. Brigid uses her divine powers to either protect the innocent or to combat evil. In this chapter we'll discuss some of the most interesting and the most unusual miracles which have been attributed to Brigid.

Vanquishing Satan

One evening Brigid and some of her nuns visited a companion who lived outside of Kildare. As they sat down to dinner, the host noticed that Brigid was looking to the side of the table and staring intently at what appeared to be nothing. She asked Brigid if something was wrong. Brigid informed everyone that Satan was standing to the side of the table watching them.

He appeared to Brigid as a beast with smoke coming from his mouth and nostrils. She demanded why he sought to corrupt the human race. He snarled and said "That the race may not attain unto Paradise."[62] She then asked what he was doing at the home of a nun and in the presence of virgins. He told Brigid that there was a certain maiden in her company who was secretly filled with "gluttony and lust."[63] It was with this woman that Satan resided.

Upon hearing this, Brigid turned to the culpable nun and made the sign of the cross in front of the woman's face. The nun immediately saw Satan standing in front of her and she was terrified. She fervently vowed to Brigid that she would change her ways and purify her thoughts. After this vow was made Satan vanished from the room and never troubled Brigid or her maidens again.

Love Potion

The *Book of Lismore* contains a story about a man who came to Brigid and begged for a miracle to save his marriage. The man's wife would not share a meal or a bed with him and she had every intention of divorcing him.

After listening to the man's plea, Brigid took a vessel of water, blessed it and handed it to him. She told the man to return home and sprinkle the water throughout the house and over his wife's food before dinner. He complied with Brigid's directions and "when he had done thus, the wife gave exceeding great love to him, so that she could not keep apart from him...she was always at one of his hands."[64]

The potion worked so well, in fact, that one morning the man left his home before his wife awoke. She panicked when he was not by her side and she raced out of the house to find her love. She found him standing on the other side of a river and threatened to jump into the water and swim across (or die trying) if he did not return to her immediately. Unfortunately, the story ends without telling us how the couple was reunited.

Confronting Violent Pagans

One day as Brigid was preaching she saw nine men who were members of a "diabolical superstition." According to Cogitosus,

The men were shouting in grotesque voices and appearing to be utterly insane. They destroyed and injured people and things in their path. The men were making wicked oaths to their god. They wanted bloodshed and planned for killing and murder of people before the calends of the next month.[65]

Brigid confronted the men and pleaded with them to stop their violence. She asked them to think of those they were harming and to find in their hearts some sympathy and compunction. The men refused stating that they must fulfill their vow to murder the innocent.

To thwart their crime Brigid made an apparition of a man which appeared before the nine men. They murdered the apparition with their lances. When this was done they drew their swords and cut off the victim's head, showing both the severed head and bloody weapons to all who stood nearby. After the "murder" was completed the men felt that their pagan vowed had been fulfilled. Brigid never ceased praying for these men. They soon repented for their deeds and were converted to the Christian faith.

The Silver Brooch

Cogitosus tells the story of a highborn yet deceitful man who had "a burning lust for a woman."[66] He devised a plan to make this woman his slave so that "he could then use her sexually as he wished."[67]

He lent an expensive silver brooch to the naïve woman on the condition that it must be kept safe and returned to him whenever he requested it. The woman agreed to these terms and thus the trap was set. The man patiently waited for the woman to leave jewelry unattended. When the moment was right he secretly stole the brooch and threw it into the sea.

The following day he appeared at the woman's home and demanded that she return what was borrowed. The woman tearfully told him that the brooch had been stolen and that she had no means of repaying him. With feigned indignation the man told the woman that, since she had lost his valuable brooch and had to money to compensate him, she must now be bound to him as his slave.

The terrified woman managed to escape from the man's custody before he could lay his hands on her. She ran to Brigid's church, "the safest place of refuge" on the island.[68] Brigid rushed to meet with the woman and offer help. The woman began to tell Brigid what had happened. Before she finished speaking a man arrived at the monastery with a fish he just caught in a nearby river. When the man cut open the belly of the fish, an expensive silver brooch rolled out onto the table.

The next day Brigid appeared at the village assembly that was meeting to determine the woman's fate. Brigid brought the brooch with her and the people at the meeting affirmed that the brooch was indeed the one that the woman borrowed. She was released from any obligations she had to the brooch's owner and she remained with Brigid from then on as one of her followers.

"Mary of the Gael"

When Brigid was a young woman still living with her father, a pious neighbor invited her to attend the Synod of Leinster.

During the synod a Bishop named Ibor was telling the assembly that the previous night he had a dream. In his dream he saw the Virgin Mary appear before them at the meeting. Just then the doors of the church opened and Brigid entered the room. The priests and bishops present took this as a sign of Brigid's holiness and from that day on referred to her as "Mary of the Gael."

The Pregnant Nun

This story is one of the most peculiar told by Cogitosus. A young nun came to Brigid seeking help. "The woman had weakened and lapsed into youthful concupiscence, as a result of which her womb had begun to swell with pregnancy."[69]

Brigid then "blessed" the woman and the child that was growing inside the womb disappeared. Thus, Cogitosus tells us, "the woman was healed without any of the pain of childbirth and she returned to penitence."[70]

Healing Lepers

Brigid did all that she could for those suffering from leprosy. She gave them shelter, food, ale, livestock, and even items of luxury. As we discussed earlier, she gave her father's valuable sword to a leper who happened to be walking past. On other occasion, she acquired the King of Leinster's armor and gave it to a leper.

Although Brigid cared for these unfortunate souls, she did not allow them to take advantage of her generosity. For instance, a "haughty" leper once showed ingratitude after receiving a cow from Brigid. Shortly thereafter the leper took his cow to the riverside. While beside the water the cow fell over and pinned the leper underneath the current where he quickly drowned.

Changing Water into Ale

In the New Testament, Jesus turned water into wine to provide for a wedding celebration. In a similar way, Brigid changed water into ale on several important occasions.

During Brigid's youth, one of her first miracles was changing water into ale for her nurse. The nurse had become ill on a journey and badly needed something to drink. Brigid took water which was unsanitary and blessed it. The foul water miraculously turned into fresh ale which quickly restored the nurse to excellent health.

Brigid also turned water into ale for her maidens, Bishop Mel, and the King of Leinster. She even performed this miracle to supply ale for her entire congregation on Easter Sunday.

Chapter 14: Brigid's Death and Relics

Brigid passed away with Ninnid by her side sometime around 525. She was buried at Kildare along with Conleth and their graves became an attraction for faithful Catholics throughout Ireland and the rest of Europe. At some point, probably in the eighth century, shrines were built for the two saints. These shrines were made of gold and silver and decorated with precious stones. The shrines were illuminated by lamps made of gold.

Around the year 800, Vikings began attacking the coastal towns of Ireland. They raided Kildare in 831 but Brigid's remains had been removed in anticipation of the attack. Her body was brought to Downpatrick Cathedral in the north of the island where it was buried alongside Saint Patrick and Saint Columba in an unmarked grave. This was done with the intention of keeping the relics safe from plunder. Unfortunately the location of the graves was soon lost. Exactly why the location was lost is unknown but it seems likely that those entrusted with the secret were either killed or carried off by the Vikings.

The location of Ireland's patron saints remained a mystery for the next three hundred years. Those living at Downpatrick knew that the bodies were buried somewhere on the church grounds. But no one knew where to look until one night in 1185 when the Bishop of Down, a man named Malachy, was praying alone in the church. Malachy begged the Lord to send some sign directing him to the sacred relics. When Malachy finished his prayer he opened his eyes and lifted his head. Before him a beam of light shone brightly in the dark church illuminating a section of the floor. The floor was dug up and the saints were at last found. They lay side by side in three simple coffins with Saint Patrick in the middle.

With the help of the Lord of Down and Pope Urban III the bodies were properly enshrined in June of 1186. The relics and the shrine remained at Downpatrick Cathedral for nearly 400 years. Sadly the shrine was destroyed by Lord Leonard Grey, the Lord Deputy of Ireland appointed by King Henry VIII.

Although the shrine was gone, Brigid's remains were saved and secretly transported to the continent. They were brought to Austria where only Brigid's skull was preserved.   In 1587, the emperor of Austria gave the skull to a Spanish clergyman living in Vienna. The clergyman brought the relic to Spain and it was later given to a Jesuit order in Lisbon, Portugal. The relic remains in Portugal and is currently housed in the Church of St. John the Baptist.

Chapter 15: Brigid's Legacy

Brigid's church became one of the leading religious institutions in Ireland. According to Cogitosus, Kildare was "the head of almost all the Irish churches with supremacy over all the monasteries of the Irish."[71] Kildare's fame and prestige grew as Irish monks traveled extensively in Europe during the Middle Ages.

In 1540, however, the Brigidine order was disbanded as part of Henry VIII's Reformation of the Church of Ireland. For more than 250 years the order that Brigid founded disappeared from history.

On February 1, 1807, the Brigidine Order was reestablished by the Bishop of Kildare, Daniel Delany.

Delany was an Irishman educated and ordained in France. When he returned to Ireland in the late 1700s he found a country devastated by colonial Britain's political and social policies. Crime, poverty, and illiteracy prevailed in Ireland's rural areas. In 1777 Delaney became a minister in Tullow, County Carlow. He was 30 years old.

Aside from his ministerial work, Delany sought to enrich the lives of his parishioners with education and music. With the help of the few literate men and women in the community, he established a Sunday school, a church choir and even a small circulating library within the parish. His success continued and by 1788 he was appointed Bishop of Kildare.

Delany's greatest contribution to both Irish and Catholic history was the re-establishment of the Brigidine Order. It began with only six Tullow women aged 25 to 48. Their names were Catherine Doyle, Eleanor Dawson, Margaret Kinsella, Judith Whelan, Bridget Brien, and Eleanor Tallon.

Bishop Delany made every effort to link this Brigidine Order with its predecessor. He emphasized at its commencement, which took place on Saint Brigid's Day, that he was not founding a new order of nuns but restoring the original Brigidine Order which the Reformation extinguished.

As a symbolic gesture of this continuity, Delany took an oak sapling from the monastery at Kildare and planted it at his new convent in Tullow.

The Tullow convent was on leased land and tree planting was strictly prohibited. As Bishop Delany and his nuns planted the oak sapling, the landlord approached and demanded an explanation. "What!" he exclaimed. "Planting trees, Sir?" To which Bishop Delany responded "With your permission, of course." Then with a smile he added "We have presumed the permission."[72]

Both the oak-sapling and the Brigidine Order grew with time. At first the order sent its nuns to assist small parishes around Tullow. Then, in 1883, a bishop in New South Wales, Australia sent a letter to the convent asking for help with the education of young Catholics in his diocese. Six nuns were sent in response to the letter. Over the next decade, the Brigidine Order expanded quickly in Australia. Its nuns were active in at least eight Australian dioceses and by 1898 the order had crossed the Tasmanian Sea and began laying foundations in New Zealand.

Despite their early achievements in Australia and New Zealand, the Brigidine nuns did not establish themselves in the United Kingdom and America until the middle of the twentieth century.

In 1948 the sisters were invited to start a school in Windsor, England. The school was a success and, about ten years later, they opened another in Liverpool. By the 1980s and 1990s members of the

Brigidine Order were living and working throughout England.

The sisters crossed the Atlantic in 1953 and founded a community in San Antonio, Texas. From there they expanded throughout the United States. Today their strongest presence is still in San Antonio, Texas with additional orders in Wilmington, Delaware and Boston, Massachusetts.

Outside the English-speaking world, the Brigidine order may be found in places as diverse as Mexico, Kenya, and Papua New Guinea. Currently, there are about 800 Brigidine sisters worldwide and nearly a hundred churches and chapels are named in honor of Saint Brigid.

Brigid's perpetual fire, extinguished in the sixteenth century, was relit in 1993 by the head of the Brigidine sisters. Since then the flame (or an artificial version of it) has burned in the center of Kildare's Market Square. It's tended by nuns of the Brigidine order as the original fire was in Brigid's time. According to an official statement from the Brigidine sisters, "The flame burns as a beacon of hope, justice and peace for Ireland and our world."[73]

About the Author

Hello and thank you for reading my book! I'm an amateur writer and history buff from Massachusetts, USA. I have two beautiful daughters, Margaret and Brigid. My wife, Maura, is an Irish dance teacher and I practice law. If you have comments about the book, I'd love to hear them. Please contact me at justin@jrmccarthy.com.

---

[1] *Book of Lismore*, Passage 1192.

[2] Kitto, H.D.F. *The Greeks* (London, 1951), p. 83.

[3] Piggott, Stuart, *The Druids* (London, 1968).

[4] Collis, John, *States without Centres.*

[5] Simon James, *The Atlantic Celts Ancient People of Modern Invention.*

[6] John Davis, *A History of Wales* (London, 1993), p. 22.

[7] Strabo, *Geography*, Book IV, Chapter 4, Passage 2.

[8] Tacitus, *Agricola*, Passage 24

[9] Cassius Dio, *Roman History*, Book LXXII

[10] Davies, Norman, *The Isles*, (New York, 1999), p. 49-50.

[11] Tacitus, Passage 21.

[12] Duffy, Kevin, *Who Were the Celts?*, (New York, 1996), p. 28.

[13] Gerald of Wales, *The History and Topography of Ireland*, Passage 71

[14] Strabo, Book 4, Chapter 4, Passage 6.

[15] Diodorus Siculus, *Library of History*, Book 5, Passage 28.

[16] Id., Passage 29.

[17] Herm, Gerhard, *The Celts*, (New York, 1975), p. 10.

[18] Julius Caesar, *The Conquest of Gaul*, Book 6, Section 2.

[19] *Cattle Raid of Cooley*, Book 14b.

[20] Wright, Brian, *Brigid: Goddess, Druidess and Saint*, (Gloucestershire, 2009), p. 7.

[21] Squire, Charles, *Celtic Myth and Legend*, (Mineola, NY, 2003), p. 63.

[22] Pliny the Elder, *Natural History*, Book 16, Passage 95

[23] Diodorus Sicilus, *Library of History*, Book 5, Passage 31.

[24] See Wright p. 23.

[25] Tacitus, *Annals of Imperial Rome*, Chapter 12.

[26] Muirchu, *Life of Patrick*, Chapter 10.

[27] Prosper, *Chronicles of Prosper of Aquitaine*, Entry for Year 431 AD.

[28] Muirchu, Chapter 8.

[29] Saint Patrick, *Confessions*, Passage 1.

[30] Id., Passage 16.

[31] Id., Passage 18.

[32] Id.

[33] Id., Passage 23.

[34] Id., Passage 55.

[35] Id., Passage 38.

[36] Acts 2: 41-42).

[37] *Confessions*, Passage 42.

[38] Pope Gregory I, *Epistle 11*, Passage 56.

[39] *Book of Lismore*, Passage 1161.

[40] Id., Passage 1192.

[41] Id., Passage 1220.

[42] Id., Passage 1231.

[43] Id., Passage 1308.

[44] Id.

[45] Lebar Brecc, Life of Brigid.

[46] Id.

[47] Id.
[48] Id.
[49] *Book of Lismore*, Passage 1341.
[50] *The Old Life of Saint Brigid*, Part 1, translated by M.A. O'Brien in Irish Historical Studies, Volume 1, Number 2.
[51] *Book of Lismore*, Passage 1341.
[52] *Book of Lismore*, Passage 1689.
[53] Cogitosus, *Life of Saint Brigid*, Passage 6.
[54] Olen, Thomas, *The Church of Ireland*, (London, 1892), p. 61.
[55] Lebar Brecc, *Life of Brigid*
[56] Id.
[57] *Book of Lismore*, Passage 1543.
[58] Id., Passage 1449.
[59] Staunton, Michael, *The Voice of the Irish*, (Mahwah, New Jersey, 2002), p.50.
[60] Id.
[61] Gerald of Wales, *The History and Topography of Ireland*, Second Part, Paragraph 77.
[62] *Book of Lismore*, Passage 1402.
[63] Lebar Brecc, *Life of Saint Brigid.*
[64] Book of Lismore, Passage 1478.
[65] Cogitosus, Passage 22.
[66] Id., Passage 25.
[67] Id.
[68] Id.
[69] Cogitosus, Passage 9.
[70] Id.
[71] Wright, p. 239.
[72] Minehan, Rita, *From the Acorn to the Oak: Celebrating the Brigidine Story*, p. 15.
[73] https://brigidine.org.au/about-us/our-

patroness/brigids-light-fire/

Printed in Great Britain
by Amazon

52796698R00067